Unity in the Father, Son, & Spirit

ONE BODY

Bible STUDY

A Biblical Deep Dive into the Operations, Administrations, and Gifts from the Father, Son, & Holy Spirit

BETH CLINE

One Body - Copyright ® 2025 by Beth Cline

Published by UNITED HOUSE Publishing

All rights reserved. No portion of this book may be reproduced or
shared in any form - electronic, printed, photocopied, recording, or by any information storage or retrieval system, without prior written permission from the publisher. The use of short quotations is permitted.

All Scripture quotations, unless otherwise indicated, are taken from the Holy Bible, New International Version®, NIV®. Copyright ©1973, 1978, 1984, 2011 by Biblica, Inc.TM Used by permission of Zondervan. All rights reserved worldwide. www.zondervan.comThe "NIV" and "New International Version" are trademarks registered in the United States Patent and Trademark Office by Biblica, Inc.

ISBN -978-1-952840-68-5
UNITED HOUSE Publishing Clarkston, Michigan
info@unitedhousepublishing.com
www.unitedhousepublishing.com

Cover & Interior Design: Beth Cline

Printed in the United States of America 2025 - First Edition

SPECIAL SALES:
Most UNITED HOUSE books are available at special quantity discounts when purchased in bulk by corporations, organizations, and special interest groups. For more information, please email orders@ unitedhousepublishing.com.

I lovingly dedicate this study to my family, my Jesus ladies—Amber, Dianne, Melissa, and Miriam—my School of Saints community, and my Leanna ladies. May God receive all the glory!

As the rain and the snow come down from heaven, and do not return to it without watering the earth and making it bud and flourish, so that it yields seed for the sower and bread for the eater, so is my word that goes out from my mouth: It will not return to me empty, but will accomplish what I desire and achieve the purpose for which I sent it. You will go out in joy and be led forth in peace; the mountains and hills will burst into song before you, and all the trees of the field will clap their hands. Instead of the thornbush will grow the juniper, and instead of briers the myrtle will grow. This will be for the Lord's renown, for an everlasting sign, that will endure forever.
Isaiah 55:10-13

About this Study

As I began to learn the gifts of the Father, Son, & Spirit, I was amazed at how God had given us such beautiful gifts. My only regret was that I wished I had learned them sooner in my spiritual walk with the Lord. I know God revealed these gifts to me in His perfect timing, but I wanted to help others see how amazing our God is in giving us gifts. These gifts have been so special and helped me understand scripture better, helped me hear from God clearer, and helped me in loving others more. I realized how He made each of us unique with our own gifts in helping us on our spiritual walk with Him and leading others to Him.

I pray this study helps you!

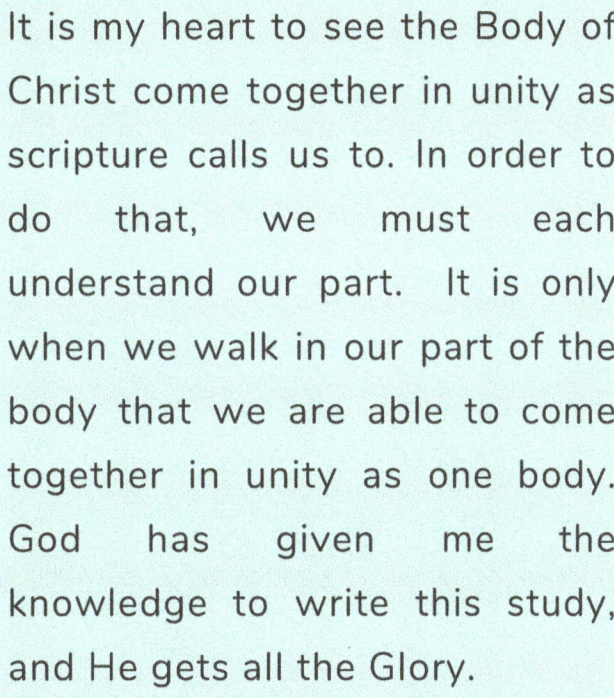

Unity in The Body

It is my heart to see the Body of Christ come together in unity as scripture calls us to. In order to do that, we must each understand our part. It is only when we walk in our part of the body that we are able to come together in unity as one body. God has given me the knowledge to write this study, and He gets all the Glory.

"There are different kinds of gifts, but the same Spirit. There are different kinds of service, but the same Lord. There are different kinds of working, but the same God works all of them in all men."
1 Corinthians 12:4-6 BSB

Love, Beth Cline

Scan with camera

The Plan

This study is a 4 Week Study

Each week you will:

1. Watch the video
2. Do the study book work
3. Answer questions
4. Spend time in the secret place
5. Reflect in your journal
6. Bonus study on page 43

Beth Cline

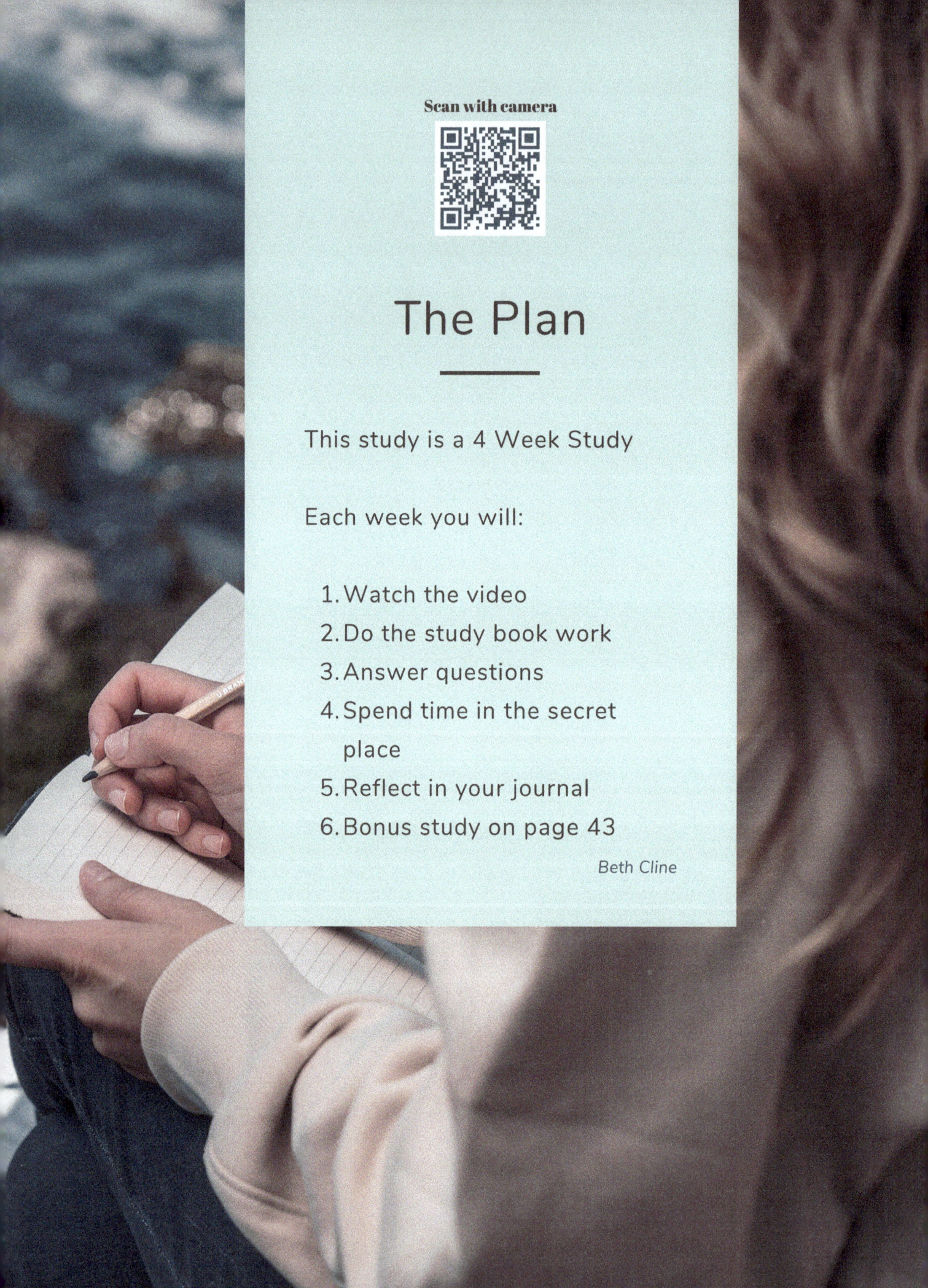

Table of Contents

06 Week One - One Body

16 Week Two - The Gifts of God

30 Week Three - The Gifts Of Jesus

42 Week Four - Gifts of the Spirit

56 Bonus - Fruit of the Spirit

60 Thank you

Week One
The Body

Scan with camera

"Ask and it will be given to you; seek and you will find; knock and the door will be opened to you."

MATTHEW 7:7

Testimony

"How have I not known about this?" I asked myself back In 2020 as God began to teach me according to His Word about the gifts of the Father, Son, and Spirit. I grew up in the church where some of these gifts were taught but not in entirety. I also began to realize that these gifts were for today! I took an incredible online class called School of Saints, led by an amazing Australian named Bianca Serratore. During these zoom calls, with ladies from across the world, I realized I was not the only one learning about these beautiful gifts for the first time. Women all over the earth were also being led by God to discover more about these gifts. The more I asked, the more the Lord began to show me. He is such a good God!

09 | One Body

How Do We Become One Body?

> **Look up 1 Corinthians 12:4-6. This scripture will help us throughout the study!**

The Father, The Son, & The Spirit

We learn from these verses that the Father gives each of us different kinds of working, but all from the same God. Jesus gives us different kinds of service, but all from the same Lord. The Spirit gives us different kinds of gifts, but from the same Spirit.

When we learn this, we can begin to open our hearts to these different kinds of Operations, Administrations, & Gifts. We also learn how the Father, Son, and Spirit distribute these gifts to us. When we begin to walk in these amazing gifts, we begin to learn our part as the body of Christ. As we will see later in this study, it is important for each of us to walk out our part. When we do this, we are able to come together as one body functioning together!

Pray and ask God to reveal these to you as we continue in His Word!

One Body, Many Parts

The body is a unit, though it is made up of many parts; and though all of its parts; are many, they form one body . . . so it is with Christ. Let's look at the verse below to learn what Paul tells us about the body in first Corinthians 12:12.

> **Now there are diversities of gifts, but the same Spirit. And there are differences of administrations, but the same Lord. And there are diversities of operations, but it is the same God which worketh all in all.**
>
> **1 Corinthians 12:4-6, KJV**

Paul goes on to say, *""Even so the body is not made up of one part but of many. Now if the foot should say, "Because I am not a hand, I do not belong to the body," it would not for that reason stop being part of the body. And if the ear should say, "Because I am not an eye, I do not belong to the body," it would not for that reason stop being part of the body. If the whole body were an eye, where would the sense of hearing be? If the whole body were an ear, where would the sense of smell be? But in fact God has placed the parts in the body, every one of them, just as he wanted them to be. If they were all one part, where would the body be?"*

1 Corinthians 12:14-19 NIV

	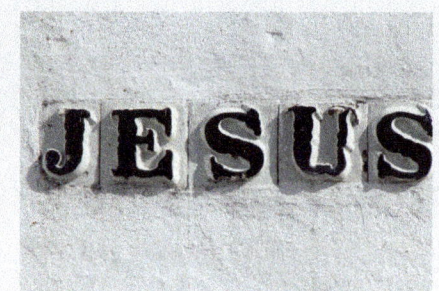	
# God	# Jesus	# Spirit
(Love and Serve)	(Church)	(Power)
Operations	Administrations	Gifts
Prophesying	Apostles	Wisdom
Serving	Prophets	Knowledge
Teaching	Evangelists	Miracles
Encouraging	Pastors	Faith
Ministry	Teachers	Healing
Giving		Prophecy
Leadership		Discernment
Mercy		Tongues
		Interpretation of Tongues

Lets look at these verses now to get an overview: We read about the operations of the Father in Romans 12:3-8, the administrations of Jesus in Ephesians 4:11-16, and the gifts of the Spirit in 1 Corinthians 12:4-11.

Have These Stopped?

We find our answer in Ephesians 4:11-13

So Christ himself gave the apostles, the prophets, the evangelists, the pastors and teachers, to equip his people for works of service, so that the body of Christ may be built up <u>until</u> we all reach unity in the faith and in the knowledge of the Son of God and become mature, attaining to the whole measure of the fullness of Christ.
Ephesians 4:11-13, emphasis added.

Has this happened?

I think we all can agree that the whole body of Christ has not come together in unity and does not have the full measure and knowledge of Christ. Therefore, we see these operations, administrations, & gifts should continue until those things do happen according to scripture.

Wrap-Up

How does the body come together in unity?

What has to be reached in order for these gifts to stop?

What three types of gifts do we have?

Spend time in the Secret Place asking God what He wants you to focus on?

There is neither Jew nor Gentile, neither slave nor free, nor is there male and female, for you are all one in Christ Jesus.

GALATIANS 3:28

Secret Place Revelation

Week Two
The Gifts of God

For you created my inmost being; you knit me together in my mother's womb.

PSALM 139:13

Testimony

As I began to learn about the gifts of God, it became clear to me that He had intentionally created me to be an encourager. I love to cheer other people on and help them see who their Heavenly Father designed them to be. It's natural for me to show everyone how special they are and how God created them to be unique.

Before I studied and understood these gifts more, I didn't realize that from the time God knitted us together in our mother's womb, He created us with these gifts. He still leaves me in awe!

We have different gifts, according to the grace given to each of us.

ROMANS 12:6

According to Grace

The Gifts of God to Love and Serve

God's Working Operations or Gifts

What gifts has God graced you with?

Let's Begin with the Administrations of God...

As we read in Romans 12:3-8, we see these gifts include prophecy, ministry, teaching, exhortation, giving, leadership, & mercy.

These workings are distributed by the Father as He creates us. These gifts are motivational gifts or our God-given gifts. We are born with these things, and they come natural to us.

Let's look at what these workings include and what they mean:

Workings	Meaning
Prophecy	Edify the body
Ministry	Service
Teaching	Teach scripture
Exhortation	Encouraging
Giving	Cheerful giver
Leadership	Take charge
Mercy	Compassion

For by the grace given me I say to every one of you: Do not think of yourself more highly than you ought, but rather think of yourself with sober judgment, in accordance with the faith God has distributed to each of you. For just as each of us has one body with many members, and these members do not all have the same function, so in Christ we, though many, form one body, and each member belongs to all the others. We have different gifts, according to the grace given to each of us. If your gift is prophesying, then prophesy in accordance with your faith; if it is serving, then serve; if it is teaching, then teach; if it is to encourage, then give encouragement; if it is giving, then give generously; if it is to lead, do it diligently; if it is to show mercy, do it cheerfully.

ROMANS 12:3-8 BSB

Prophecy

Prophecy is a gift from God. We see prophecy throughout the whole scripture. You may think of Joseph and his prophetic dreams. Moses heard from God and even went up on the mountain to talk to God. Moses was a seer and a hearer. We also see in scripture where Rahab knew the spies were sent from God and how to help them. Some may even have a feeling that God is trying to tell them something. In Amos 3:7 it says, "Surely the Sovereign Lord does nothing without revealing his plan to his servants the prophets."

Prophecy is always for building up and edifying the body of Christ. Prophecy will always be confirmed in scripture according to God's Word and should always align with the Father's heart.

Ministry

The gift of ministry is a gift to serve the sheep. Like David served, we must also serve. Many that have this gift enjoy helping others. Whether it be listening or praying for others, there are many acts of service according to the Father's heart.

Galatians 5:13 says, "You, my brothers and sisters, were called to be free. But do not use your freedom to indulge the flesh; rather, serve one another humbly in love."

Teaching

Teaching is a gift God gives us to help others learn the Word of God, and the person typically has a deep understanding of scripture.

"All Scripture is God-breathed and is useful for teaching, rebuking, correcting and training in righteousness, so that the servant of God may be thoroughly equipped for every good work." 2 Timothy 3:16-17

We should use all teaching according to the Word of God and in alignment with scripture. We should teach in love and point everyone to the Father, as He is the best teacher.

Exhortation

The gift of exhortation is to encourage others in love.

"Therefore encourage one another and build each other up, just as in fact you are doing." 1 Thessalonians 5:11

Exhortation is reminding God's children who they are in Christ and encouraging them in the Lord, emphasizing how good our Father is and what His Word says.

Giving

Scripture says that we should be cheerful givers. The Father gives this gift so we can have a cheerful heart as we give and take care of others just as He cares for us.

2 Corinthians 9:7 says, "Each of you should give what you have decided in your heart to give, not reluctantly or under compulsion, for God loves a cheerful giver."

We should give just as the Father so generously gives to us. Do you enjoy giving to others? If so, you may have the Father's gift of giving.

Leadership

"Not lording it over those entrusted to you but being examples to the flock."
1 Peter 5:3 NIV

We should lead as Jesus did. As leaders, we may be in charge, but we should lead by example. Jesus is our example of leading with humility, love, and honesty.

Mercy

Our Heavenly Father is merciful. He sacrificed His only Son for us. Having the gift of mercy is having compassion for others. Matthew 5:7 tells us, "Blessed are the merciful, for they shall receive mercy."

Let's Ask God

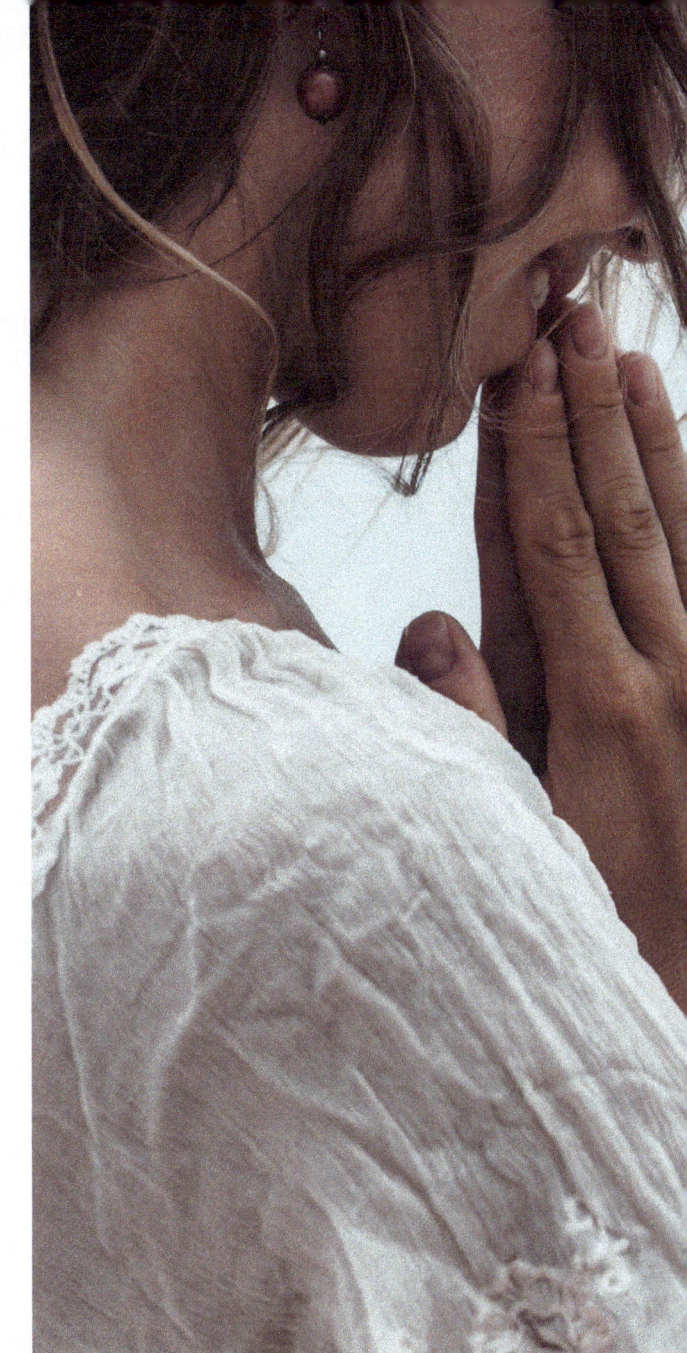

Pause, pray, and ask God to reveal to you what gifts He has graced you with. You may already know or have an idea but ask Him how He would like to use these gifts in you! He is such a good Father and gives generously.

> Take this time in the Secret Place to thank God in advance for these gifts.

1. What did God reveal to you?

2. What did you learn about the Gifts of God?

Wrap-Up

What Operational gift do you most relate with?

How can you use this gift to help others?

What are all of the gifts of God?

Have you ever taken a gifts quiz?

Every good and perfect gift is from above, coming down from the Father of the heavenly lights, who does not change like shifting shadows.

JAMES 1:17

Secret Place Revelation

Week Three
The Gifts of Jesus

Scan with camera

The stone the builders rejected has become the cornerstone.

PSALM 118:22

Testimony

When learning about the gifts of Jesus, I loved that scripture points out that Jesus is our head, and we are the body of Christ. I began to realize I have an apostolic gifting. This is why I have built my own business (with God leading, of course). It is also why I dream big and can see the vision for things. I know they will happen, but I am not always sure of the details on how to get there. I also love helping people find their gifts. I feel it helps people to understand how amazing Jesus is and that He wants us to be willing vessels to help unite and build up the body of Christ.

I began wondering why we don't see all five of these gifts in the church?

The Gifts of Jesus

We learn about the gifts or administrations of Jesus in Ephesians 4:11-16. These gifts can also become offices of the body of Christ. Many have the giftings of these offices without ever being called to use them in ministry. However, these giftings help build the body of Christ into unity when we walk these out.

> *Jesus is the head of the body.*

So Christ himself gave the apostles, the prophets, the evangelists, the pastors and teachers, to equip his people for works of service, so that the body of Christ may be built up until we all reach unity in the faith and in the knowledge of the Son of God and become mature, attaining to the whole measure of the fullness of Christ."
Ephesians 4:11-13

To Achieve Unity

The Gifts of Jesus for the Church/Body of Christ

The Gifts of Jesus

The following are the gifts of Jesus according to scripture:

Apostle - build-up ministries and the body of Christ, plant churches, want to see others working in their giftings, and dream big with God.

Prophets - bring the word of the Lord to the body of Christ, encourage and build up the body of Christ.

Evangelist - preach, equip, and gather, have a heart for souls saved, and to spread the gospel

Pastor - train and build up, care and shepherd the flock.

Teacher - teach the Word of God and have a deep understanding of scripture.

Many in the body have these gifts and do not feel called to an office. Some are called to an office in the church. My question when learning about these gifts were why do we often only see three of these offices in the church? Shouldn't we see all five gifts in the church?

Each gift must flow from :

LOVE

Let's look back at Ephesians 4:14-16

Then we will no longer be infants, tossed back and forth by the waves, and blown here and there by every wind of teaching and by the cunning and craftiness of people in their deceitful scheming. Instead, speaking the truth in love, we will grow to become in every respect the mature body of him who is the head, that is, Christ. From him the whole body, joined and held together by every supporting ligament, grows and builds itself up in love, as each part does its work.

Every gifting must flow from LOVE

Ask the Lord!

Take this time in the secret place, which means anywhere alone, and ask the Lord Jesus Christ to reveal to you what your gifts are. Ask Him how he wants to use you to build up the body of Christ. Thank Him for being our head!

Let's Reflect

When we operate in any of our gifts, from what should they always flow?

Wrap-Up

What are the gifts of Jesus for?

What gift(s) of Jesus do you relate the most with?

Jesus answered, 'I am the way and the truth and the life. No one comes to the Father except through me.'

JOHN 14:6

Which of these offices do you see in your church?

Do you feel called to an office in the church?

Secret Place Revelation

Week Four
The Gifts of the Spirit

Scan with camera

"May the God of hope fill you with all joy and peace as you trust in him, so that you may overflow with hope by the power of the Holy Spirit."

ROMANS 15:13

Testimony

Before 2020, I had heard of the gifts of the Spirit mentioned, but I'm not sure I really understood them. I very rarely saw them in operation. When I began to pray about these gifts and ask the Holy Spirit to give me what He thought I needed, I didn't know what to expect.

One night, shortly after I began asking the Spirit to teach me, I asked God a question and had a dream with the answer. He even gave me scripture to confirm what I saw in my dream. Wow! My first prophetic dream from God. I was excited to learn more about these gifts. Next, the Lord showed me to pray for someone who was sick. I did, and 4 months later she was healed! God didn't need me, but how cool that He let me be a part of this gift of healing.

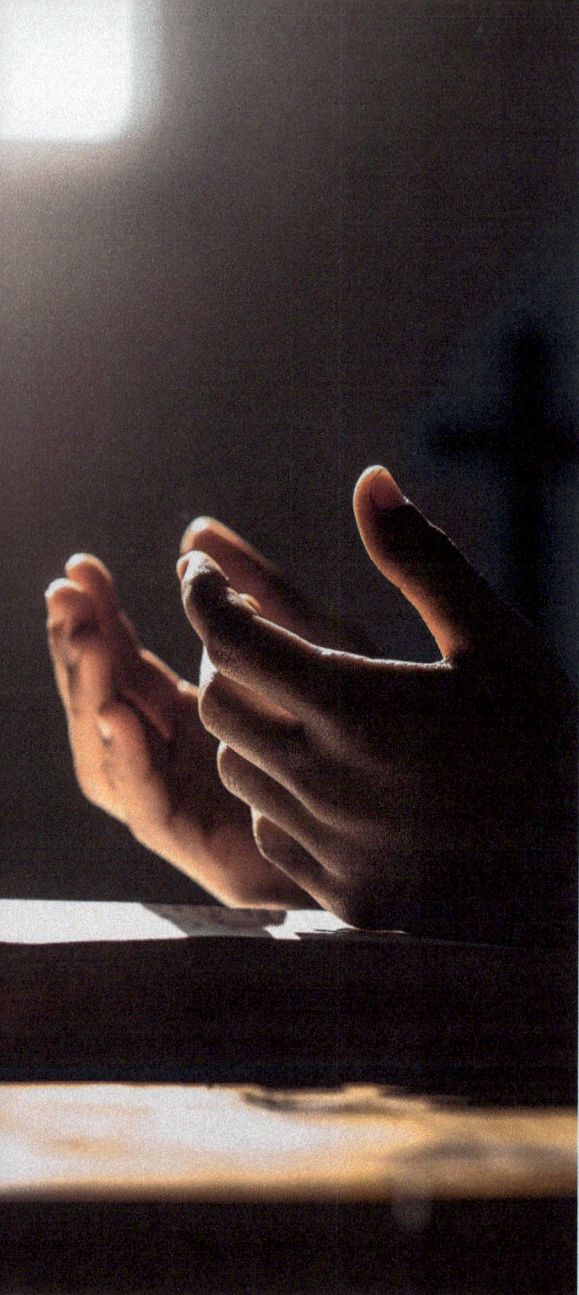

The Spirit

Turn in your Bible to
1 Corinthians 12:7-11

We see in these verses that the Spirit distributes these gifts just as he determines . . .

Here are the Gifts of the Spirit according to these scriptures;

Wisdom - uses the Word to guide them.

Knowledge - insight into past and present revealing something to minister or discern.

Faith - gift of bold faith and believing.

Healing - healing the sick.

Miracles - signs and wonders.

Prophecy - edify and exhort the body (all are called for this gift).

Discernment - to discern the spirits.

Tongues - spirit in a heavenly language for praising and/or warfare.

Interpretation - interprets the heavenly language of tongues.

Follow the way of love and eagerly desire spiritual gifts, especially the gift of prophecy.

1 CORINTHIANS 14:1

For the common good

The Gifts of the Spirit for Power

More on the Spirit

We see in 1 Corinthians 14:1 that Paul tells us we should all desire the gifts of the Spirit, especially the gift of prophecy. I was truly shocked when reading this because we hear so little about this gift today. Paul reminds us in the Word that we should desire this gift of prophecy because it helps to build up and edify the body of Christ! What should it always be done in?

| LOVE |

Prophetic gifting

The gift of Prophecy includes seers, hearers, knowers, and feeler.

seer
You may receive dreams and visions from the LORD as a seer.

hearer
You may hear God speak directly to you as a hearer.

knower
You may have an inner knowing from God to direct you as a knower.

feeler
You may feel things in the spiritual atmosphere as a feeler.

All prophecy should align with scripture and the Father's heart.

Ask The Spirit

Now, take time to ask the Spirit of God to fill you. Tell Him that you desire the gifts He has for you! Ask Him to reveal the gifts He so freely gives and ask the Holy Spirit to help you use these gifts according to God's Word.

Unique Gift

Which gift is included in all three gifts of the Father, Son, & Spirit?

PROPHECY

The gift of Prophecy is the only gift that is given by every member of the trinity!

Is this why Paul tells us in 1 Corinthians 14:1 "Follow the way of love and eagerly desire spiritual gifts, especially the gift of prophecy?"

This gift is used to edify and build up the body of Christ.

Even on my servants, both men and women, I will pour out my Spirit in those days, and they will prophesy.

ACTS 2:18

Revelation

I feel it is important to share the revelation God showed me while learning these gifts through scripture. I am sure we have all heard the popular verse in 1 Corinthians 13:4-13. It starts with:

Love is patient, love is kind . . .

Please go read 1 Corinthians chapter thirteen starting in verse one. Paul is explaining to us what love is and isn't. Why?

> **To tell us how we should only use our gifts in love!**

Let's read 1 Corinthians Chapter 13 in its entirety!

1 Corinthians 13

If I speak in the tongues of men or of angels, but do not have love, I am only a resounding gong or a clanging cymbal. If I have the gift of prophecy and can fathom all mysteries and all knowledge, and if I have a faith that can move mountains, but do not have love, I am nothing. If I give all I possess to the poor and give over my body to hardship that I may boast, but do not have love, I gain nothing. Love is patient, love is kind. It does not envy, it does not boast, it is not proud. It does not dishonor others, it is not self-seeking, it is not easily angered, it keeps no record of wrongs. Love does not delight in evil but rejoices with the truth. It always protects, always trusts, always hopes, always perseveres. Love never fails. But where there are prophecies, they will cease; where there are tongues, they will be stilled; where there is knowledge, it will pass away. For we know in part and we prophesy in part, but when completeness comes, what is in part disappears. When I was a child, I talked like a child, I thought like a child, I reasoned like a child. When I became a man, I put the ways of childhood behind me. For now we see only a reflection as in a mirror; then we shall see face to face. Now I know in part; then I shall know fully, even as I am fully known. And now these three remain: faith, hope and love. But the greatest of these is love.

Love never fails

May the God who gives endurance and encouragement give you the same attitude of mind toward each other that Christ Jesus had, so that with one mind and one voice you may glorify the God and Father of our Lord Jesus Christ.

ROMANS 15:5-6

Wrap-Up

What are the three different types of gifts?

How would you describe the Gifts of God?

How would you describe the Gifts of Jesus?

How would you describe the Gifts of the Spirit?

*All Gifts should flow from _____.

Why does Paul tell us what love is in Chapter 13 in 1 Corinthians?

Which gift should we all desire?

How do we become one body?

All of the gifts should _____ and _____ the body of Christ.

Secret Place Revelation

You will know them by their :

Fruit

Paul tells us in Galatians, we who belong in Christ Jesus no longer walk in the flesh, but by the Spirit. When we walk in the Spirit, we will have good fruit that others will know us by. These fruits must be used when operating in the gifts of the Spirit. We cannot prophesy, teach, heal, etc. without walking in the fruit of the Spirit. Therefore, we must check our hearts before we share a word, knowledge, exhort, etc. We must have the Father's heart to walk in the Spirit. So, what does the fruit of the Spirit include?

But the fruit of the Spirit is love, joy, peace, patience, kindness, goodness, faithfulness, gentleness, self-control; against such things there is no law.
Galatians 5:22-23

Let's Reflect

What are the Fruit of the Spirit?

1. _____
2. _____
3. _____
4. _____
5. _____
6. _____
7. _____
8. _____
9. _____

Read Galatians chapter five & inscribe it on your heart.

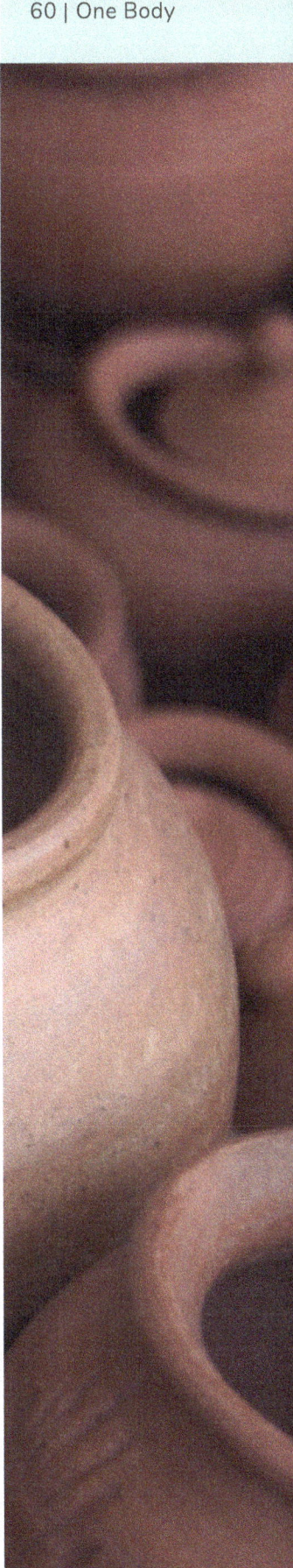

Thank You!

I want to thank each of you for joining us on this study! My prayer is that we lean closer into the Lord and become the spotless bride of Christ as one body to prepare for His return. I want to thank God for leading me on this journey, and He gets all the Glory!!

I also want to thank all those who have helped me grow in the Lord! Thank you to my family, friends, School of Saints, my Leanna ladies, and Jesus ladies!

My prayer is that God will use you as a vessel and impart you with the gifts as He sees fit. He isn't looking for a perfect vessel but a willing vessel with a pure heart.

> **May God bless each of YOU!**

About The Author

God-made, Jesus-saved, and Kentucky-raised, Beth Cline is fiercely passionate about helping others discover and walk confidently in their God-given identity. Rooted in Scripture and led by the Spirit, Beth teaches with clarity and conviction on the importance of knowing who we are in Christ, activating spiritual gifts, and boldly advancing the Kingdom of God.

Teaching on spiritual gifts—and intentionally exploring her own—has become both a personal calling and a professional mission. As the owner, founder, and CEO of Leanna Cosmetics, Beth leads her company with a foundation in biblical principles, stewarding her platform with excellence and integrity.

Under the Lord's direction, she also founded Kingdom Marketing, The Glory Television Network, and hosts the annual *Glory Event*—a powerful gathering of believers hungry for the presence of God. Through speaking engagements, Bible studies, and media, Beth equips others to step into their God-ordained purpose with courage and joy.

Beth cherishes time with her husband, Mike, and their beautiful children. When she's not ministering, you'll likely find her at the lake, cheering at a hometown football game, or spending quiet time in the secret place with the Lord, where every good work is birthed.

www.ingramcontent.com/pod-product-compliance
Lightning Source LLC
Chambersburg PA
CBHW040010080526
44586CB00028B/2947